My First Joke Book

Scoular Anderson

YOUNG CORGI BOOKS

MY FIRST JOKE BOOK
A YOUNG CORGI BOOK : 0 552 54278 4

First published in Great Britain by Young Corgi Books 1986
This edition published 1998

PRINTING HISTORY
First edition reprinted 1988, 1990, 1992, 1994

Text and illustrations copyright © Scoular Anderson 1986

The right of Scoular Anderson to be identified as the author of this work has
been asserted in accordance with the Copyright, Designs and Patents Act 1988

Young Corgi Books are published by Transworld Publishers Ltd,
61-63 Uxbridge Road, Ealing, London W5 5SA,
in Australia by Transworld Publishers (Australia) Pty. Ltd,
15-25 Helles Avenue, Moorebank, NSW 2170,
and in New Zealand by Transworld Publishers (NZ) Ltd,
3 William Pickering Drive, Albany, Auckland.

Made and printed in Great Britain by
Cox and Wyman Ltd, Reading, Berkshire.

My First
Joke Book

For Kirsty and Kathala

Where do snowmen dance?

At the snowball.

David: It's raining cats and dogs.

Tracy: I know, I've just stepped in a poodle.

How can you tell if there's an elephant in your fridge?

Footprints in the butter.

How can you tell if there's an
elephant in your oven?

You can't get the door shut.

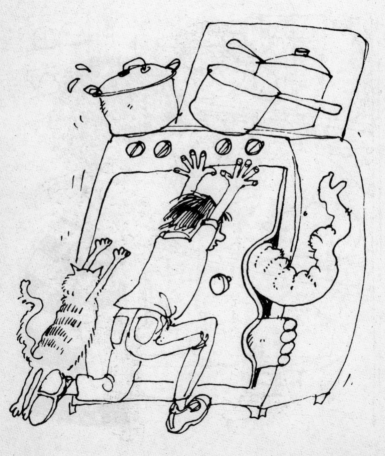

Doctor, doctor, I feel like a pair of curtains!

Oh, pull yourself together, boy!

Doctor, doctor, I keep thinking
I'm a spoon.

Well sit there and don't stir.

Knock knock.

Who's there?
Irish stew.

Irish stew who?
I arrest you in the name of the law.

Knock knock.

Who's there?

Someone who can't reach the bell.

What reptiles are good at doing sums?

Adders.

What kind of tiles can't be stuck on walls?

Reptiles.

What's the difference between a jeweller and a jailor?

One sells watches and the other watches cells.

What's the difference between a wet day and a lion with toothache?

One pours with rain and the other roars with pain.

Why does the ocean roar?

Because it has crabs on its bottom.

Why is the sea friendly?

Because it's always
giving little waves.

Waiter, your thumb's in my soup!

Don't worry madam, it's not hot.

Waiter, what is this fly doing in my soup?

Looks like the breast-stroke, sir.

What do you call an eskimo's cow?

An eskimoo.

How does the eskimo stick his
house together?

With iglue.

Why is it dangerous to walk on grass with bare feet?

Because it's full of blades.

KEEP OFF THE GRASS

What sort of shoes are made out of banana skins?

Slippers.

How do you start a teddy-bear race?

Ready, teddy, go!

How do you start a jelly race?

Get set!

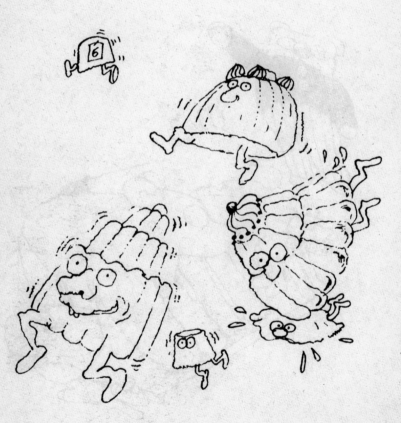

What happened to the little girl who slept with her head under the pillow?

The fairies took all her teeth away.

Why are false teeth like stars?

Because they come out at night.

What did the string of pearls say to the hat?

You go on ahead, I'll just hang around.

What did one ear say to the
other ear?

Between you and me,
we need a hair cut.

What is the crocodile's favourite game?

Snap!

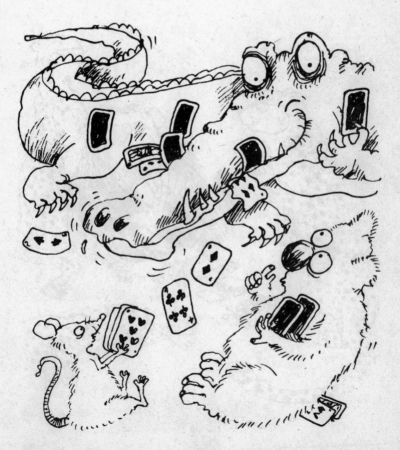

Why is it difficult to play cards in the jungle?

There are too many cheetahs.

What's white on the outside and green on the inside and hops?

A frog sandwich.

Why are cooks so cruel?

Because they beat the eggs and whip the cream.

What's bad-tempered and goes with custard?

Apple grumble.

What goes straight up in the air and wobbles?

A jellycopter.

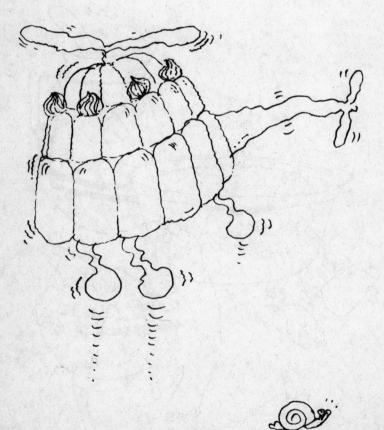

What did the father ghost say to his son?

Spook only when you're spooken to.

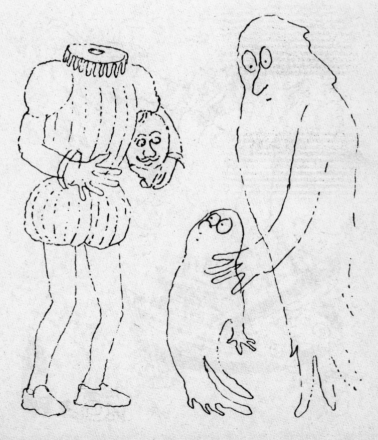

What do sea-monsters eat?

Fish and ships.

What animal do you look like when you have a bath?

A little bear.

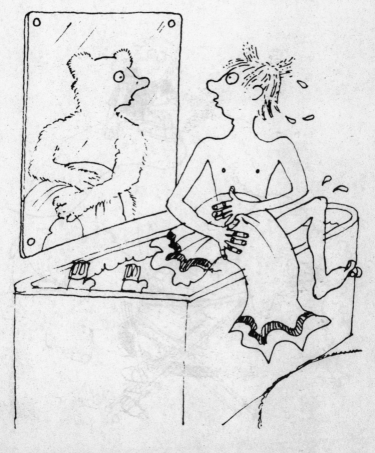

Why are elephants grey and wrinkled?

Because they are so difficult to wash and iron.

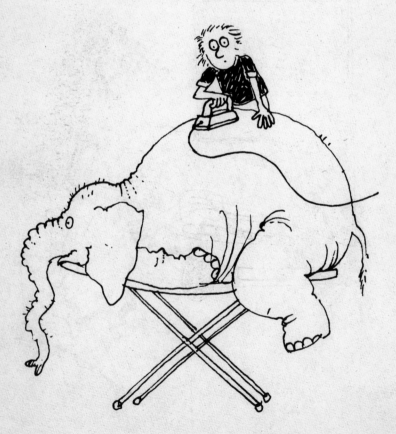

What did the traffic lights say to the car?

Don't look now, I'm changing.

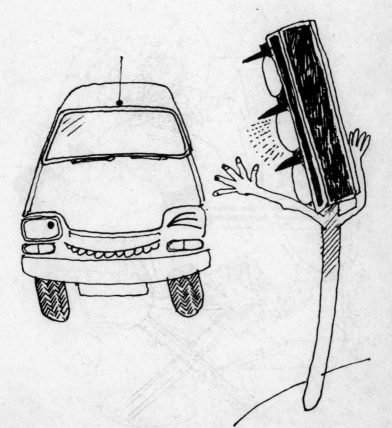

What's another name for a dentist's surgery?

A filling station.

What's green and goes boing-boing?

Spring cabbage.

What's green and hairy and goes up and down?

A gooseberry in a lift.

What did the man say when he robbed a glue factory?

This is a stick-up!

Why did the robber take a bath?

So he could make a clean getaway.

What is yellow and dangerous?

Shark—infested custard.

What else is yellow and dangerous?

A canary with a machine-gun.

How do you know if there's an elephant under the bed?

Your head touches the ceiling.

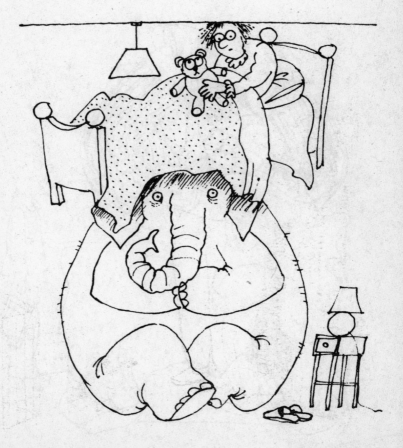

How do you know if there's an elephant in your bed?

You can see the 'E' on his pyjamas.

Why do witches fly on broomsticks?

Because vacuum-cleaners are too heavy.

What kind of witches are found in the desert?

Sandwitches.

What did the big chimney say to the little chimney?

You're too young to smoke.

What goes ninety-nine bonk?

A centipede with a wooden leg.

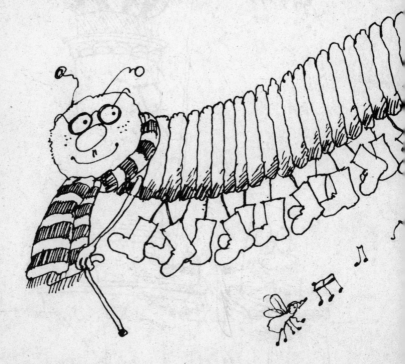

Why do bees hum?

Because they don't know the words.

What did the big candle say to the little candle?

I'm going out tonight.

Did you hear about the two flies playing football in a saucer?

They were practising for the cup.

Why is a football stadium so cool?

Because it's full of fans.

Why do rabbits have shiny noses?

Because their powder puffs are at the wrong end.

What do you get if you pour boiling water down a rabbit hole?

Hot cross bunnies.

What animal is grey, has four legs and a trunk?

A mouse going on holiday.

What animal is grey, has four legs, a long nose and is very large?

A big, long-nosed mouse.

How do fishermen make nets?

They sew lots of holes together.

How do you keep a skunk from smelling?

Hold its nose.

Why are dogs like trees?

They both have barks.

What happened to the cat who
swallowed a ball of wool?

She had mittens.

What do you give a sick lemon?

Lemon aid.

What do you give a sick bird?

Tweetment.

Why is a barn so noisy?
Because cows have horns.

What do you call a sleeping bull?

A bulldozer.

What is black and white and red all over?

A sunburnt penguin.

What is black and white and read all over?

A newspaper.

Jane: Mum, I've knocked down the ladder outside.

Mum: Well, don't bother me, tell Dad.

Jane: He already knows, he's hanging from the roof.

Tommy: Mum, Granny's sitting watching the washing machine.

Mum: Well, there's nothing wrong with that.

Tommy: But she thinks she's watching wrestling on T.V.

Why did the chicken cross the road?

To get to the other side.

Why did the turkey cross the road?

It was the chicken's day off.

Where do astronauts leave their spacecraft?

At parking meteors.

What did the spaceman see in his frying pan?

An unidentified frying object.

What did the stamp say to the envelope?

Stick with me and we'll go places.

What has sixty keys but can't open any doors?

A piano.

Doctor, doctor, I feel like a bell.

Give me a ring when you feel better.

Doctor, doctor, I feel like a window!

Where's the pane?

Shall I tell you the joke about the high wall?

I'd better not, you'd never get over it.

Shall I tell you the joke about the body snatchers?

I'd better not, you might get carried away.

Here are some pages for your own jokes!

For Your Own Jokes

For Your Own Jokes

For Your Own Jokes

THE ALIEN JOKE BOOK

by John Byrne

What do space monsters have on their toast?
Mars-malade.

Look out – the aliens are coming!
Space monsters, robots and those little
green men from Mars – they're on their
way with spaceships full to bursting with
the most HILARIOUS jokes from
outer space EVER.

The JOKES are out there...

0 552 545462 7

LONG TALES, SHORT TALES AND TALL TALES

by Colin West

Francis was a special pig, whose snout was small, but brain was big...
It wasn't long before this porker had turned into a super talker!

Chuckle at the tale of Francis, a talking porker who has a way with words. Chortle as you discover how a sheriff deals with Bert, the dirtiest cowboy in the West – and howl as you meet a pirate with *seriously* smelly feet. These, and many other hilarious characters, are packed into this fabulously funny collection of story poems – some long, some short and some *very* tall!

0 552 52798 X

IF YOU ENJOYED THIS BOOK, YOU MIGHT ENJOY ANOTHER TITLE FROM YOUNG CORGI AND CORGI BOOKS

Joke books

0 552 545058	THE HAUNTED JOKE BOOK	John Byrne	£2.99
0 552 545627	THE ALIEN JOKE BOOK	John Byrne	£3.99

Poetry

0 552 527092	A STACK OF STORY POEMS	Tony Bradman	£3.99
0 552 528005	DIRTY GERTIE MACKINTOSH	Dick King-Smith	£3.99
0 552 52798X	LONG TALES, SHORT TALES AND TALL TALES	Colin West	£3.50

Short stories

0 552 545376	A BOX OF STORIES FOR 6 YEAR OLDS	Pat Thomson	£3.99
0 552 52817X	A BARREL OF STORIES FOR 7 YEAR OLDS	Pat Thomson	£3.99
0 552 527300	A SACKFUL OF STORIES FOR 8 YEAR OLDS	Pat Thomson	£3.50

All Transworld titles are available by post from:

Book Service By Post, PO Box 29,
Douglas, Isle of Man, IM99 1BQ

Credit cards accepted.
Please telephone 01624 675137, fax 01624 670923
or Internet http://www.bookpost.co.uk or e-mail: bookshop@enterprise.net for details

Free postage and packing in the UK.
Overseas customers: allow £1 per book (paperbacks) and £3 per book (hardbacks).